What really happened
and why it really matters

Carl Laferton

the**good**book
COMPANY

For Suzy and Sam,
with thanks for letting me use your parents'
house to write this book.

Easter Uncut

© The Good Book Company, 2016.

The Good Book Company
Tel: 0333 123 0880; International: +44 (0) 208 942 0880
Email: info@thegoodbook.co.uk

Websites:
UK: www.thegoodbook.co.uk
N America: www.thegoodbook.com
Australia: www.thegoodbook.com.au
New Zealand: www.thegoodbook.co.nz

ISBN: 9781909919310

Design by André Parker
Printed in the UK

Contents

Introduction

I recently found a diary that I kept for a month while I was at college.

As I remember it, my life at 19 was exciting, and I was interesting. But the evidence remembers it a bit differently. In truth, life was quite dull, and I was quite dim.

So 19-year-old Carl wakes up late because he went to sleep late simply because he couldn't be bothered to go to bed, and then records that he is very tired and needs more sleep. He lazes around most days, and then one day a week records that he worked "extremely hard" (four hours in a single day) because a work deadline was looming. Then he writes that he must be more organised, before repeating the same timetable the week after.

And, apart from watching lots of sport (on a TV or from the substitutes' bench), and spending a fair amount of money he didn't have on things he didn't need, that's life. Quite dull, and fairly dim.

Not your average week

Most of our diaries would be similar, I'd imagine. Things happen, life goes on its way, resolutions come and go, mistakes get made but not learned from... and then there's the odd burst of great joy, or worry, or grief. That's ordinary life—a large amount of mundane details, punctured by the odd life-changing event.

But every now and then, an ordinary person finds themselves at the centre of extraordinary events. The diary of someone who marched with Martin Luther King, or who lived in 1945 Berlin, or who worked for King Henry VIII, would be fascinating—not because of who the writer is, but because of what they saw, who they were with, and what they were part of.

This book is about a diary. Thankfully for all of us, the diary is not mine. It's the account of a man called John who lived in the first century, grew up as a fisherman, met someone who changed his life, and wrote down what happened next. And the part we're focusing on is a week in which John witnessed loyalty, arguments, betrayal, love, desertion and injustice; a week of great plans, shattered dreams, nightmare scenes and renewed hope.

It was not your average week. It was the week in history that we now call "Easter".

Eggs or execution?

Easter is strange, when you think about it. On the one hand, there are fluffy bunnies and lots of eggs. On the other, there is a man being brutally executed. Since it's hard to wrestle both those images into the same story, we tend to focus on the fluffy bits and cut out the execution part.

But this book doesn't. In fact, it ignores the bunnies. That's because John is writing down what really happened in history—the version of Easter that comes with an 18-certificate, and is much more interesting for it. In each chapter, you'll read ▶ **What really happened**—what John saw. In each of these sections, you'll see some words in **this kind of text**. Those are taken straight out of the Bible, and are the really important ones. Those in normal text are written by me, just to help you grasp what was going on.

But John's diary doesn't only tell us what happened in all its gripping twists and turns. It also shows us ▶ **Why it really matters**. The man who changed John's life was Jesus, a carpenter who claimed to be a king, and who still grabs the attention and draws the devotion of millions of people even today, 2,000 years later. As you'll see, John tells us far more about Jesus than he does about himself. In fact, when he refers to himself, he doesn't even use "I" or his own name—he describes himself just as "the disciple Jesus loved".

In each chapter, you'll read one of John's entries about this strangest, most disturbing and thrilling of weeks. And you'll read about why those events back in distant history still live on—how they can change your own life and future.

Not many diaries are very interesting—mine certainly isn't. But this one is. Not many lives matter 2,000 years later—mine certainly won't. But this one does.

Welcome to Easter—uncut.

1. Saturday night. Dinner with friends.

❯ What really happened

Six days before the Passover, the greatest festival of Israel's year, **Jesus came to Bethany,** a village a short distance from the capital, Jerusalem. This was **where Lazarus lived, whom Jesus had** recently **raised from the dead. Here a dinner was given in Jesus' honour.** Lazarus' sister **Martha served, while Lazarus was among those reclining at the table with him.**

Then Mary, Lazarus' other sister, **took about half a litre of pure nard, an expensive perfume; she poured it on Jesus' feet and wiped his feet with her hair. And the house was filled with the fragrance of the perfume.**

But one of his disciples, Judas Iscariot, who was later to betray him, objected, "Why wasn't this perfume sold and the money given to the poor? It was worth a year's wages."

He did not say this because he cared about the poor but because he was a thief; as keeper of the disciples' **money bag, he used to help himself to what was put into it.**

"Leave her alone," Jesus replied. "It was intended that she should save this perfume for the day of my burial. You will

* Words straight from the Bible are **in this kind of text**.

always have the poor among you, but you will not always have me."

Meanwhile a large crowd of Jews—the people who lived in Israel—found out that Jesus was there and came, not only because of him but also to see Lazarus, whom he had raised from the dead.

READ THE FULL STORY John 12 v 1-9

▶ Why it really matters

I knew I loved her when I spent all my money—and a chunk of my overdraft—on her birthday present.

At the time, I'd only been dating Lizzie for a couple of weeks. Aware of my own shortcomings, I asked a friend to help me choose a suitable gift. Julia pointed to a necklace. It was stunning—and its price tag was, to a student, startling.

The normal Carl would have walked away and bought something cheaper, sensible, affordable. But something strange happened to me. I found myself in the shop, credit card in hand, buying this necklace. I didn't even pause to calculate how many nights out or tickets to the football it was costing me. I bought it.

It was at that moment that I realised I was in love.

The best thing I have...

You can tell what you truly love by what you give to it, and what you give up for it. We all have something, or someone, we would give anything to. Why? Because we're in love. It could be an idea, an ambition, a job, a possession, a person. It could, of course, be yourself. There will be something.

And as Jesus pauses in Bethany on his way into Jerusalem—and on the way into the hardest week of his life—John records for us an act of true love, of overwhelming generosity. As Jesus ate with his closest friends, "Mary took about half a litre of pure nard, an expensive perfume; she poured it on Jesus' feet and wiped his feet with her hair".

In that culture, it wasn't strange to put perfume on a man's feet; it was a place of dusty roads and open sandals, and male feet are not known for being naturally sweet-smelling. What is strange—startling—is the type and amount of perfume Mary used. It was worth a year's average salary. She was effectively pouring 5,000 five-pound notes or ten-dollar bills—over a man's feet. Me putting my credit card onto the jewellery shop's counter has nothing on this.

Mary is saying to Jesus, in a stunning, perfumed way: *I love you. The best thing I have is this perfume, and it's yours. You are worth it.*

I am worth it

It is startling. But even more startling is how Jesus responds. I don't know what picture of Jesus you have in your head—but most people think that, if he did exist, he was a reasonable, humble kind of guy. So what do you expect him to say, as someone gives him a present they can't really afford?

"You shouldn't have. No, really, you shouldn't have."

But he doesn't say that. When others object, and point out that if Mary didn't want the perfume for herself, she could at least have sold it and given the money to the poor, Jesus doesn't agree. No: "Leave her alone," he replies.

Mary thinks Jesus is worth everything—more worthy even than helping the poor. And Jesus agrees. "You will always have the poor among you," he says, "but you will not always have me." He's saying: *Yes. I am worth it.*

It's a claim of staggering audacity—arrogance, even. How do you respond? To be honest, I want to respond as Judas does:

"Why wasn't this perfume sold and the money given to the poor?"

It's a very good point.

Money talks

But John, as he records this event, knows Judas better than that. Actually, it isn't lifting poor people from poverty that Judas cares about; it is lining his own pockets to increase his prosperity. What does Judas love? Money. Judas is focusing on the money-bag, because that's where he'll find all he needs. It's worth bending a few rules (John would call it thieving; Judas would call it being savvy) in order to grab some more money. It's what he loves.

You can tell as you read John's entry whose side he is on here, and it's not Judas'. But it's worth asking, *Whose side am I on?* Do you line up with Mary, pouring out everything she has because she thinks Jesus is worth it? Or with Judas, seeking to maximise his own wealth because he thinks money is worth it? To put it another way, if Jesus were here now, would you set up a direct debit to divert your whole salary, for twelve months, into his bank account?

No? Neither would I. Unless... unless he really is worth it. What if Jesus offers something that money can't buy, which Judas won't find in the moneybag and we won't find in our bank balance?

Worth it?

The answer to that question is not found by looking at Mary wiping the perfume with her hair, nor at Judas grumbling as he counts the cost to his personal wealth, nor at Jesus telling Judas to leave Mary alone. It's found by looking at another member of the dinner party.

A strange thing happens at the end of the dinner. A large crowd come to have a look. Eating dessert is not usually a spectator sport—but this dinner is different. The crowd of locals are there "to see Lazarus". They want to gawp and gaze at Mary's brother.

Why?

Because last time many of them had seen him, he hadn't been lying beside a table, eating, as was the fashion in this outpost of the Roman empire. He'd been lying in a tomb... dead.

So they came to see Lazarus, whom "Jesus had raised from the dead". Jesus had stood at the tomb of this man and he had wept tears at his friend's death, just as we all do when a loved one dies. Then he had said, "Lazarus, come out!" (John 11 v 43). And Lazarus had come out, this dead man, now alive.

When we look at Lazarus, alive and eating, suddenly Mary's actions don't seem so extravagant or over the top. Jesus had given her brother his life back. He had cancelled her grief. The guestlist of this dinner was literally miraculous. Of course Mary would give everything she had to Jesus, because he had given her so much more.

That's love. That's why I spent my overdraft on Lizzie's birthday present. Deep down I had a sense that whatever I gave to her, she would give more back to me—that whatever I gave up for her, it would always be worth it, because I was getting *her*.

That's why Mary spent so much on Jesus. And that's why Christians today spend their lives on Jesus. You're probably reading this book because you know a Christian who is normal in most ways, but sometimes does things that are at best confusing and at worst crazy. They give up money, time or energy that they could use to enjoy themselves. They are willing to miss out on a promotion or a pay-rise, on being respected or having a relationship. They are willing to say things that aren't popular. They're normal in many ways, but strange in some.

They're like Mary. They've discovered that when you give everything to Jesus, he gives back far more.

Second best

Judas never discovered that. He loved money more than he loved Jesus. He followed Jesus around, but Jesus was a sideshow to him—not the main event. If he was around today, Judas would have gone to church at Christmas and Easter—Jesus was welcome to have those times of the year. Perhaps he'd have given Jesus his

Sunday mornings, too. But he wouldn't have given Jesus his life. Monday mornings would have been about getting money, about grabbing the life that he wanted and that a good income would buy him.

And the irony is that because Judas held back, he missed out. He missed out on all that Jesus would give—on life, on an end to grief, on hope and security for the future. He ended up with second best—and, within a week, he ended up with nothing at all.

What are you aiming for in life? Could it be that you're settling for second best? Could it be that what you love most can't give you as much as Jesus can?

Jesus thinks so. He thinks he's worth everything. That's either breathtaking arrogance, or it's breathtakingly accurate. The events of the next few days would first suggest that Jesus couldn't have been more wrong about himself—and then make plain that he couldn't have been more right.

A house full of...

So, as Mary wipes up the perfume, Judas stares angrily at the money bag, and the villagers all gaze at the risen Lazarus, what strikes John is that "the house was filled with the fragrance of the perfume". But it's not just sweet fragrance the house is full of.

It's full of questions: Is Jesus really worth it? Is Mary being sensible, or stupid?

It's also full of tension—because Jesus doesn't only tell Judas to leave Mary alone. He adds that "it was intended that she should save this perfume for the day of my burial". Whether she knew it or not, Mary was preparing a corpse for burial. Jesus is saying, *Look at Lazarus. He was recently dead. Now look at me. I soon will be.*

2. Sunday. To the city.

▶ What really happened

As Jesus ate with Lazarus, Mary, Martha and his disciples, the Jews of the village weren't the only ones interested in what was going on.

The chief priests—the religious leaders—were also keeping an eye on events. They had recently met together to discuss the threat Jesus posed to them, because **many of the Jews who had seen what Jesus did** for Lazarus **believed in him.**

One of them, named Caiaphas, who was high priest that year, said to them: **"It is better for you that one man die for the people than that the whole nation perish." So from that day on they plotted to take** Jesus' **life.**

But on that Friday night, as they considered the events in Bethany, the religious leaders realised that they had an additional problem: Lazarus—the walking, talking evidence of Jesus' power. **So the chief priests made plans to kill Lazarus as well, for on account of him many of the Jews were going over to Jesus and believing in him.**

The next day the great crowd that had come to the capital—to Jerusalem, which was also known as Zion—to celebrate the Passover **festival heard that Jesus was on his way to**

Jerusalem. They took palm branches and went out to meet him, shouting,

"Hosanna!"

"Blessed is he who comes in the name of the Lord!"

"Blessed is the king of Israel!"

Jesus found a young donkey—a colt—and sat upon it, as it is written in the Jews' holy writings, the Scriptures:

"Do not be afraid, Daughter Zion;
see, your king is coming,
seated on a donkey's colt."

At first his disciples did not understand all this. Only after Jesus was glorified—after the events of the next week had passed—did they realise that these things had been written about him and that these things had been done to him.

Now the crowd that was with him when he called Lazarus from the tomb and raised him from the dead continued to spread the word. Many people, because they had heard that he had performed this sign, went out to meet him. So the Pharisees—a particular group of religious leaders—said to one another, "See, this is getting us nowhere. Look how the whole world has gone after him!"

READ THE FULL STORY John 11 v 45-53; 12 v 10-19

> Why it really matters

Some species of animals have better public relations departments than others.

Take lions, for instance. At some point, someone somewhere decided they should be known as "King of Beasts". When we think lion, we think (unless we happen to be antelopes) strong, brave, majestic.

Or bears. Bears—who in reality are aggressive killers—are seen as cuddly, cute and a comforting image for a small child's toy.

Or reindeer. Their marketing department came up with the genius idea of linking their fortunes to Santa's sled. Then they invented Rudolph. Suddenly reindeers stopped being boring animals who live in cold wastelands. Now they are heroes, loved by children and sung about each Christmas.

On the other hand, there are cockroaches. Despite the fact that they are adaptable, resourceful and one of the few species who could breed quickly enough to survive a nuclear holocaust, not many people like them. No one gives their child a cuddly cockroach toy. They need better PR.

And then, somewhere in between lions and cockroaches, you have donkeys. Solid, dependable, humble, workmanlike, dull, possibly (thanks to Winnie the Pooh, whose author was clearly doing PR for the bears) sad, and probably a bit clumsy.

That's what we think when we hear or read the word *donkey.* Plodding… dull… solid, but unspectacular.

And that means that when we read what John saw on a Sunday morning 2,000 years ago, it is completely natural for us to get totally the wrong end of the stick as we read that in order to ride into Jerusalem, "Jesus found a young donkey and sat upon it".

And it's therefore very easy for us to be swayed by the donkeys' bad PR as we read what the crowds shouted as he rode in: "Blessed is the king of Israel!"

What kind of king rides a donkey?! Presumably a nice, unspectacular, dull one.

But don't be fooled. Jesus chose to ride a donkey to say the exact opposite of that. In first-century Israel, clambering onto a donkey to enter the capital city meant something very different, and much more exciting.

Who rides a donkey?

Jesus didn't pick the donkey because it happened to be available. He chose it because he wanted to point people watching to what was "written" in their holy writings: "Do not be afraid, Daughter Zion; see, your king is coming, seated on a donkey's colt."

Jesus is saying, or rather showing, that the crowds have got one thing right: that he is a king. By riding the donkey, he is making a statement: *Your king is coming.*

But he's doing more than that. Because John didn't write out everything that "is written"—everything that one of Israel's prophets, the people Israel regarded as a mouthpiece of God, had uttered 600 years before. Here's what Zechariah said—or rather, what God said through Zechariah (and what every Jew lining the roads as Jesus passed would have known by heart). As you read it, think about what kind of king Jesus is claiming to be.

"Rejoice greatly, Daughter Zion!
 Shout, Daughter Jerusalem!
 See, your king comes to you,
 righteous and victorious,
 lowly and riding on a donkey,
 on a colt, the foal of a donkey.
 I will take away the chariots from Ephraim [another name for Israel]
 and the war-horses from Jerusalem,
 and the battle-bow will be broken.
 He will proclaim peace to the nations.
 His rule will extend from sea to sea
 and from the River to the ends of the earth.
 As for you, because of the blood of my covenant with you,
 I will free your prisoners from the waterless pit."

(Zechariah 9 v 9-11)

The King Zechariah is talking about is neither unspectacular, nor dull. This King is all-powerful, and his rule is all-encompassing—he will rule "from sea to sea", over an empire greater than any the world has ever seen. This King is all-conquering—his people won't need to fight their own battles, because he'll fight and win their battles for them. He will bring peace to the world, and freedom to his people. This King will be all-perfect—he will be "righteous" in all he says, decides and does.

How do you spot this King? Zechariah gave just one sign: he would be riding a donkey as Jerusalem shouted joyfully about him. Now, centuries later, a man who had just freed a friend from the grave reached the outskirts of Jerusalem, "found a young donkey and sat upon it".

That man was saying, *Read Zechariah's prediction about a coming king. Then look at me on the donkey.*

I am that King. I have come to start building my kingdom, and one day my kingdom will cover every inch of this world.

The King you want

So if you'd been there that Sunday morning, you wouldn't have seen a plodding animal. You'd have seen a limousine, a tank and a throne all rolled into one and given four legs. You'd have seen a means of transport fit for the greatest US President or the most powerful British monarch.

You'd have seen King Jesus—all-powerful, all-encompassing, all-perfect, come to bring victory and freedom and peace to his subjects.

And even though you weren't there that morning, it is still great news for you that God has sent a King like this. First, it allows us to be optimistic about the future. One day, Jesus will rule from sea to sea; he will proclaim peace, and there will be no more fighting or need for fighting. What an optimistic view of the world's future!

And we all need this kind of hope. Without hope, we're just existing. But I'd suggest that as we look at our world—and, when we're honest, at our own lives—there are more grounds for pessimism than for hope. As peace comes to one place, war breaks out in another. As one politician promises great things, another makes a catastrophic error of judgement. As we get one thing right, we get another thing wrong. Yet still we cling to the idea that tomorrow might just be better than today—because without hope, we're just existing.

As King Jesus rides his donkey, he says: *A day is coming that will be infinitely, and permanently, better than today. No more terror. No more errors. No more let-downs. No more wrong.*

Second, as Jesus rides his donkey, he offers us clarity about life. We only have one life each, none of us can see what lies ahead, and many of us know that there are other people who depend on our decisions and efforts. It's quite scary when you think about it. Life is like driving in the dark with broken headlights and no satnav or map. But here is a leader who can tell us what life is about. We can be confident that his directions are the best route to follow. We don't need to hope for the best; we can *know* what is best.

Third, as Jesus rides his donkey, he tells us our longings are right. As you look at the conflicts around you and within you—on the pages of the newspaper, maybe in your own family, probably in your own heart—don't you long for peace? Whenever you realise that you're trapped by a decision you once made and can't undo… or by a mistake you regret but can't make up for… or by a decision that someone else made and you are suffering for… don't you long for freedom? As King Jesus rides his donkey, he says, *That's why I've come—to use all my power to proclaim peace and bring freedom.*

As we start to realise that Jesus is that King, it makes sense of how the crowds reacted. They heard he was coming and they went to meet him, shouting "Hosanna", a word that means "Give us rescue now!"—*King Jesus, we need your peace and freedom.* They recognised him, and they welcomed him into their city.

Count us out

But not everyone did. John records not only the highlights of the day, but also the dark clouds. Not everyone saw Jesus' ride on a donkey as good news. To some, it was deeply threatening. The religious leaders had opposed Jesus from the very start of the three years he had spent explaining and proving that he really was God's promised, all-powerful, all-perfect King. They had resolved to kill him, to crush his popularity. Yet here he was, being welcomed by the people—by "the whole world", as they put it with some exaggeration.

So as Jesus rides into Jerusalem, the religious leaders are not welcoming him—they are seeking to wipe him out. Why? Why would they do that, when his coming is such great news? Because if Jesus is in charge, then they are not. If Jesus is the King, then people will praise him, and not them.

The leaders didn't like Jesus because they loved being praised and they loved having power. The King's arrival threatened that. And his arrival still does today. For those who love their reputations and want to be in charge, Jesus will always be an unwelcome intruder. And there's a little part (or a large part) of each of us that lines up with these religious leaders, whether we consider ourselves religious or not. We like to be in charge, rather than under Another's rule. We like to earn people's praise, rather than seeking to give it to Another.

And so we are in a strange position. We need God's King to come and rule. We long for the hope and clarity and peace and freedom he brings. And yet, naturally, you and I find it uncomfortable, even threatening, to hear that there is an all-powerful, all-encompassing, all-victorious King—and that it's not us.

In a way, it would have been easier for us if Jesus had never raised Lazarus from the dead and never got on that donkey—if he had never claimed and proved that he was this King. But he did. That's challenging. But at the same time, it's wonderful. There is a King.

There is a kingdom. And because he has come in the past, his kingdom will come in the future, bringing at last the peace and freedom we all long for.

Unless, of course, the religious leaders get their way, and the King on the donkey becomes a corpse in a tomb.

3. Thursday night. Staying in.

▶ What really happened

It was just before the Passover festival. Jesus knew that the hour had come for him to leave this world and go to the Father. Having loved his friends, he loved them to the end.

The evening meal was in progress, and the devil had already tempted Judas, the son of Simon Iscariot, to betray Jesus. Jesus knew that the Father had put all things under his power, and that he had come from God and was returning to God; so he got up from the meal, took off his outer clothing, and wrapped a towel round his waist. After that, he poured water into a basin and began to wash his disciples' feet, drying them with the towel that was wrapped round him. This was a job only performed by foreign slaves.

He came to one of his disciples, Simon Peter, who said to him, "Lord, are you going to wash my feet?"

Jesus replied, "You do not realise now what I am doing, but later you will understand."

"No," said Peter, "you shall never wash my feet."

Jesus answered, "Unless I wash you, you have no part with me."

"Then, Lord," Simon Peter replied, "not just my feet but my hands and my head as well!"

When Jesus had finished washing their feet, he put on his clothes and returned to his place. "Do you understand what I have done for you?" he asked them. "You call me 'Teacher' and 'Lord', and rightly so, for that is what I am. Now that I, your Lord and Teacher, have washed your feet, you also should wash one another's feet. I have set you an example that you should do as I have done for you. Very truly I tell you, no servant is greater than his master, nor is a messenger greater than the one who sent him. Now that you know these things, you will be blessed if you do them."

READ THE FULL STORY John 13 v 1-17

▶ Why it really matters

Saparmurat Niyazov renamed a city and a meteorite after himself during the fifteen years he was dictator of Turkmenistan. He renamed the month of September with the title of his autobiography. He banned dogs from his capital because he didn't like their smell. He amassed a personal fortune of over $3 billion. That's how you live if you're a despot.

The singer Mariah Carey reputedly flew her dog first-class till he grew too big for the seat—then she bought him a private jet. According to reports, she only drinks through a straw, and employs someone to hold her glass as she sips. And her bed has to be surrounded by twenty humidifier machines. That's how you live if you're a diva.

Why, if you find yourself a despot of a country or a diva in the pop charts, do you live like that? Because that's how power is instinctively used. People tend to use the power they have to serve themselves. The more power, the more self-service, and the more outrageous the lifestyle and the demands.

I like to think I wouldn't be like that if I were president of Turkmenistan, or had vocal cords that could cover five octaves. But it's more likely that the difference between me, Saparmurat Niyazov and Mariah Carey is not in how much we each like to serve ourselves, but rather in how much power we have. The fact is that I often use the power that I do have in order to serve myself. To take one example, I have power over my time at weekends. And usually, I aim to use that time to do what I want to do. In my best moments, I choose to do chores or look after the kids. But not all my moments are my best moments. More often, I use my time to serve my comfort or pleasure. All of us do, to some extent. We don't rename months or employ someone to hold our drink, but we do use the power that we have to serve ourselves.

The nineteenth-century British politician Lord Acton said, "Power tends to corrupt, and absolute power corrupts absolutely". He's right, but only half-right: in fact, power reveals corruption, and absolute power reveals absolute corruption. The way we use the power we have reveals the kind of people we are, deep down.

We've already seen the truth of this around Jesus. Judas had power over the money bag; it revealed him for what he was—a thief. The religious leaders had power over the people; it revealed them for what they were—praise-seekers.

Powerful slavery

And in the middle of all this is Jesus, claiming to be not only powerful, but all-powerful—not only a great man, but God come as a man. That's how he described himself—as possessing a level of power and an amount of possessions literally beyond our dreams. How he uses his power will reveal what kind of person he is, deep down.

So here on this Thursday evening is King Jesus in a room with his followers. They're eating their meal, but there's no one to wash their feet. Remember, this is a pre-pedicure culture, where the roads were covered in dust and animal excrement, and where people wore sandals or no shoes at all. Foot-washing was the lowest job imaginable. It was so disgusting that in Israel, slaves who had Israelite (Jewish) nationality were never required to do it; only foreign slaves were. Washing others' feet was a job that said: *I have no power. If I did, I wouldn't be doing this.*

So the group sit down to eat, without a foreign slave around to wash their feet, and suddenly the man who rode the donkey gets up, prepares the water, takes off his cloak, and begins "to wash his disciples' feet".

The all-powerful King suddenly starts acting like the lowliest slave. It is like going to a Mariah Carey concert, visiting the toilet on the way out, and finding Mariah unblocking a toilet with her bare hands. It is like walking past the White House to find the President on hands and knees, cleaning up where the local drunks had vomited the night before.

It is astonishing. Why would Jesus do such a thing? Because he wants to reveal an awesome truth, make an amazing claim, and point to a deeper need.

An awesome truth

Here's the awesome truth: the all-powerful King wants to slave for his people. There is literally nothing he won't do for his subjects. There is no job too horrendous, too difficult or too demeaning for him to take on if it will help his friends. Jesus' power does not reveal his corruption: it displays his perfection. He could have demanded his feet be washed by a disciple. As the King of everything, he could have summoned an angel to do it. He could have commanded that he be waited on. Instead, he chose to do it himself, and wash not his own feet, but the feet of others. He is that kind of leader. It's the kind of leader we may glimpse in others, or may strive to be ourselves. It's the kind of leader Jesus was, all the time, in every way. There was nothing he wouldn't do.

If you read through the whole of John's Gospel—John's record of the events he saw day by day for three years—you'll see that no matter how much pressure Jesus was under, no matter how put upon or put down or let down he was, he never acted selfishly. It is staggering to think that a life has been lived that did not involve any self-centredness, at all, in any way at any stage. What is still more staggering is that this life was lived by a man who deserved to be served and who could have demanded to be served—but he never, ever did. He always looked out for others, whoever they were, whatever they'd done, however they'd treated him. He was, and is, the all-powerful King, who always wants to slave for his people, who always does what's best for his people—even if they haven't asked him to and don't understand what he's doing.

An amazing claim

Here's the amazing claim: if you live like Jesus did, you'll be happier than if you live like divas do.

Even while I tut at the abuses of despotic tyrants and the demands of pop stars, a part of me would quite like to enjoy their lifestyle— because wouldn't it be a happy day when everything ran to my timetable, my every wish was fulfilled, my every desire was met? *No,* says Jesus! "I have set you an example that you should do as I have done for you ... Now that you know these things, you will be blessed if you do them."

To be "blessed" is to enjoy life as it was designed by God to be— full of freedom and fulfilment. Jesus' strange claim is that the path to blessing does not lie in using our power to serve ourselves, but in using it to slave for others—just as he did. He slaves for his friends; then he tells them to slave for each other.

This tips what we naturally think upside down. It goes against the way the world works and the way many of us were brought up, because it tells us that we win as we lose, that we're blessed as we slave. How can that make sense? It doesn't, unless we realise that we don't need to serve ourselves, because the all-powerful King Jesus serves us. A subject of a King who is always serving them is free gladly and voluntarily to use their power for others. There's great blessing in being free to do that.

So there's no such thing as half-hearted Christianity. I once knew a guy who said that his "Christianity" was like his golf club membership: he was a non-playing member. What he meant was that he liked the experience of church, liked the idea of eternal life and liked being around Christians; but that he himself wouldn't commit, wouldn't serve. But the King says, *Every member plays.* A non-playing member is actually a non-member. Following Jesus is about whole-heartedly seeking to serve like Jesus. It is about living in a way the world never understands—of slaving, and knowing blessing. Those who have tried it have found that it does not fail.

A deeper need

There's a strange moment as Jesus kneels to start washing Simon Peter's feet. The subject asks the King, in astonishment and disbelief, "Lord, are you going to wash my feet?" And the King says, "You do not realise now what I am doing, but later you will understand".

In one sense, Peter did understand—Jesus was washing his feet. But Peter didn't understand that Jesus was pointing him as he sat there, and John as he listened in, and us as we read today, to a deeper truth that Peter would only` understand "later". It's a truth Jesus hints at when he tells Peter, "Unless I wash you, you have no part with me". He is saying, *Unless you let me slave for you in order to wash you clean, you cannot be my subject or my friend.* Jesus is telling Peter that foot-washing, horrible though it is, is not the most horrendous thing he will go through in order to serve Peter. He is saying that Peter's feet, dirty and disgusting though they are, are not the part of him that most needs cleaning. The King will go even lower than a slave. And he will do it to clean his subjects.

Peter doesn't understand. I wouldn't have, either, if I'd been there. And maybe you don't as you read these words. But that was Jesus' point—Peter would only understand "later". The events of the next 72 hours would give Peter all the understanding he needed.

4. Friday morning. The verdict.

❯ What really happened

With feet freshly washed, Jesus and his friends began to eat their evening meal. Then Jesus said, **"Very truly I tell you, one of you is going to betray me."**

His disciples stared at one another, at a loss to know which of them he meant. Jesus told Judas, **"What you are about to do, do quickly."** But no one at the meal understood why Jesus said this to him. Since Judas had charge of the money, some thought Jesus was telling him to buy what was needed for the festival, or to give something to the poor. Judas went out. And it was night.

Jesus left with his disciples and crossed the Kidron Valley. On the other side there was a garden, and he and his disciples went into it.

Now Judas, who betrayed him, knew the place, because Jesus had often met there with his disciples. So Judas came to the garden, guiding a detachment of soldiers and some officials from the chief priests and the Pharisees.*

* John doesn't tell us what happened to Judas after this—but another disciple, Matthew, does: **When Judas, who had betrayed him, saw that Jesus was condemned, he was seized with remorse … he went away and hanged himself** (Matthew 27 v 3, 5). He had given up Jesus, and lost everything.

Peter, who had a sword, drew it and struck the high priest's servant. But Jesus commanded Peter, "Put your sword away! Shall I not drink the cup the Father has given me?"

So the detachment of soldiers with its commander and the Jewish officials arrested Jesus. They bound him and brought him first to Annas, who was the father-in-law of Caiaphas, the high priest that year.

Then the Jewish leaders took Jesus to the palace of the Roman governor. Pilate came out to them and asked, "What charges are you bringing against this man?"

"If he were not a criminal," they replied, "we would not have handed him over to you."

Pilate said, "Take him yourselves and judge him by your own law."

"But we have no right to execute anyone," they objected.

Pilate then went back inside the palace, summoned Jesus and asked him, "Are you the king of the Jews?"

"Is that your own idea," Jesus asked, "or did others talk to you about me? My kingdom is not of this world. If it were, my servants would fight to prevent my arrest by the Jewish leaders. But now my kingdom is from another place."

"You are a king, then!" said Pilate.

Jesus answered, "You say that I am a king. In fact, the reason I was born and came into the world is to testify to the truth. Everyone on the side of truth listens to me."

"What is truth?" retorted Pilate. With this he went out again to the people gathered there and said, "I find no basis for a charge against him. But it is your custom for me to release to you one prisoner at the time of the Passover. Do you want me to release 'the king of the Jews'?"

They shouted back, "No, not him! Give us Barabbas!" Now

Barabbas had taken part in an uprising.

Then Pilate took Jesus and had him flogged. He was bound to a post, stripped, and beaten with a whip that had lead balls or pieces of bone attached, which lacerated his skin. Though floggings were sometimes fatal, Jesus survived his. Then **the** soldiers twisted together a crown of thorns and put it on his head. They clothed him in a purple robe and went up to him again and again, saying, "Hail, king of the Jews!" And they slapped him in the face.

Once more Pilate came out and said to the Jews gathered there, "Look, I am bringing him out to you to let you know that I find no basis for a charge against him." When Jesus came out wearing the crown of thorns and the purple robe, Pilate said to them, "Here is the man!"

As soon as the chief priests and their officials saw him, they shouted, "Crucify! Crucify!"

But Pilate answered, "You take him and crucify him. As for me, I find no basis for a charge against him."

The Jewish leaders insisted, "We have a law, and according to that law he must die, because he claimed to be the Son of God."

When Pilate heard this, he was even more afraid, and he went back inside the palace. "Where do you come from?" he asked Jesus, but Jesus gave him no answer. "Do you refuse to speak to me?" Pilate said. "Don't you realise I have power either to free you or to crucify you?"

Jesus answered, "You would have no power over me if it were not given to you from above."

Pilate tried to set Jesus free, but the Jewish leaders kept shouting, "If you let this man go, you are no friend of Caesar, the Roman emperor. Anyone who claims to be a king opposes Caesar."

When Pilate heard this, he brought Jesus out and sat down on the judge's seat at a place known as the Stone Pavement. It was the day of Preparation of the Passover; it was about noon.

"Here is your king," Pilate said to the Jews.

But they shouted, "Take him away! Take him away! Crucify him!"

"Shall I crucify your king?" Pilate asked.

"We have no king but Caesar," the chief priests answered.

Finally Pilate handed him over to them to be crucified.

READ THE FULL STORY   John 13 v 21-22, 27-30; 18 v 1-3, 10-13, 28-40; 19 v 1-16

▶ Why it really matters

If this were a movie, tense music would play throughout this scene, as Jesus is betrayed by a friend, arrested by the guards, questioned by the chief priests, interviewed by the Roman governor, tortured, mocked by soldiers, and put on show before the Jewish leaders and the people. The music would build, until suddenly it would stop, as Pilate sits down on his judge's seat to tell the people his final verdict:

Pilate: Here is your king.

People: *Take him away! Take him away! Crucify him!*

Pilate: Shall I crucify your king?

And the chief priests would give their own final verdict:

We have no king but Caesar.

The we would see Pilate nod to the detachment of soldiers, and the beaten, bloodied man wearing a mocking crown made of jagged thorns would be hauled from the platform and dragged towards the site of his execution. And if this were a movie, the cinema-goers would shuffle uncomfortably, decide that next time they'd watch something a bit more light-hearted, and go home.

But this wasn't a movie. There wasn't any music. There were just whispered accusations, angry shouts, increasingly desperate questions, and then the last demand:

Take him away! Take him away! Crucify him!
We have no king but Caesar.

This was reality. And at the end of the scene, an innocent man was being dragged off to die.

Why?

Jesus: he's just too...

Put simply, no one wanted Jesus to be alive anymore. In claiming to be a king—and not just any king, but *the* King, the King God had promised through Zechariah—Jesus had raised the stakes. Now he had lost the game. Everyone heard of his claim to be King, and everyone said, *No.*

That day, there were three ways in which Jesus was rejected. First, there was the mockery. The soldiers simply saw a weak man claiming to be a monarch but now crushed by the real power-brokers—so they mocked him. They called him king, but only while they slapped him. He was just too *weak* to be King.

Second, there was the hatred. The chief priests had hated Jesus for years and plotted his death for months. But how could they arrest such a popular man? By finding an insider—Judas—to lead them to Jesus while it was dark and he was far from the crowds. They'd given him a quick show trial, and brought him to Pilate for what they thought would be a rubber-stamping of a sentence of execution. "He must die," they told Pilate, "because he claimed to be the Son of God". They hated Jesus too much to stop and wonder whether he might have claimed that because it was true. He was just too *threatening* to be King.

Third, there was the respect. It's possible to reject Jesus while admiring him. Pilate, the Roman governor, shows us that. Pilate knows there is "no basis for a charge against him". He says to Jesus, "You are a king, then!" He seems intrigued, even impressed, by this man who gives such deep, strange answers rather than begging for his life. But he knows that if Caesar hears that Pilate heard a man claim to be king in part of the Roman empire and did nothing to stop it, he will be in trouble. So Pilate signs the death warrant of an innocent man. Jesus is just too *inconvenient* to be King.

The soldiers, the chief priests and Pilate all decide, in the end, that there must be "no king but Caesar".

And so King Jesus must die.

Caesar, please

It's not surprising that the soldiers and Pilate chose Caesar over Jesus. After all, he paid their wages. But what is astonishing is the Jewish leaders' decision to pledge loyalty to the Roman emperor. Here was the man whose armies occupied Israel; who had taken freedom and peace away and brought oppression and death in their place. Here was the man these leaders dreamed of, and schemed about, replacing.

And they say, *We'd like him to be king, please. He's our only ruler.*

That is how determined they are to resist Jesus' right to rule. They will trade freedom and peace for oppression and death if it means getting rid of Jesus. It is a tragedy. And it is self-chosen.

Who rules?

But before we are too quick to point the finger at these chief priests, we need to see that in many ways we stand in their sandals. Each day, all of us choose whether we will be ruled by King Jesus or not. Of course, there are lots of different ways to choose *not*. But almost without noticing, *not* is what we choose, one way or another. Jesus is just too inconvenient, too threatening or too weak-looking. When we disagree with something Jesus says about how we should live in his world, we simply say, *You don't rule.* We don't scream, *Crucify him.* But we quietly insist, *Take him away.* We would rather he weren't alive and weren't ruling—and so we live as though he isn't.

Some do that with great respect. They are willing to let Jesus be a teacher, a guide, a guru—just not King. Some do it with mockery. They laugh at his followers, and try to catch him out and prove him wrong with questions. Some do it with outright hatred. They don't believe in the God who Jesus claimed to be, but they hate this God they don't believe in—they hate him for all the ways in which he is different from how they would invent him if they had the chance. Whichever we choose—whether it's respect, mockery or anger—we all say, *Take him away.*

The Bible has a simple word for rejecting the rule of Jesus. It's "sin". Sin is primarily an attitude, rather than an action. So if we all kept a daily diary, some of us would have an impressive record of a good life, lived well—a life of helping others, being kind, working hard. Others would have a deeply unimpressive record of a wasted life—a life of consistent selfishness, trampling on those around us, living off others' hard work. Most of us would have a mixture. But all of us, no matter how good or bad our deeds, would have written underneath each entry in invisible ink: *Jesus is not my King. Take him away.* If God were to read our diary, that is what he would see:

8th March: Jesus is not my King. Take him away.

9th March: Jesus is not my King. Take him away.

10th March: Jesus is not my King. Take him away.

What God doesn't do

The most chilling aspect of this miscarriage of justice is not so much what the soldiers, the priests and the governor do—it's what God doesn't do.

He doesn't stop it.

Jesus tells Pilate, "You would have no power over me if it were not given ... from above". God could stop his Son being taken away and executed—but he doesn't. He lets the people there that day make their choice. He lets them reject Jesus as their King and choose Caesar as ruler. God gives them what they ask for.

And he always has. From the very beginning of human history, God has said, *If you want to live without my King as your ruler, you will have what you want. If you want to reject peace and freedom, and choose oppression and death, I will give you what you choose.*

God still says that. He looks at our spiritual diary and he gives us what we ask for—for ever. Through Zechariah and his other prophets, God has promised that his King will rule from sea to sea—the entire world will be at peace, free from everything that is bad, bringing people all they have ever longed for, for ever. When we choose to live outside of that, God doesn't stop us. His punishment for us rejecting his Son as King is to give us eternity outside his Son's kingdom: an eternity without peace, without freedom, without our heart's longings. It's an eternity that we have chosen; but it's an eternity of regret about what we chose. It's an eternity that the Bible calls "hell".

Jesus' death shows how far sinful people will go to shut out God's King from God's world. But Jesus' death also shows how far he will go to open up his world to sinful people. As he'd told his disciples in the garden as he was arrested, Jesus viewed "the cup" of his death not as something force-fed him by guards, or religious leaders, or a Roman governor—but as something "given me" by "the Father".

Jesus wasn't going to die because other people forced him to, as the climax of their plan to get rid of him. He was going to die because he himself chose to, as the climax of God's plan to invite us in. How could that be? The events of the next few hours would show John, and us.

5. Friday midday. At the execution.

▶ What really happened

The soldiers took charge of Jesus. Carrying his own cross, he went out to the place of the Skull (which in Aramaic is called Golgotha). There they crucified him, and with him two others—one on each side and Jesus in the middle.

Pilate had a notice prepared and fastened to the cross. It read: JESUS OF NAZARETH, THE KING OF THE JEWS. Many of the Jews read this sign, for the place where Jesus was crucified was near the city, and the sign was written in Aramaic, Latin and Greek. The chief priests of the Jews protested to Pilate, "Do not write 'The King of the Jews', but that this man claimed to be king of the Jews."

Pilate answered, "What I have written, I have written."

When the soldiers crucified Jesus, they took his clothes, dividing them into four shares, one for each of them, with the undergarment remaining. This garment was seamless, woven in one piece from top to bottom.

"Let's not tear it," they said to one another. "Let's decide by lot (the first-century version of flipping a coin) who will get it."

This happened that the scripture might be fulfilled that said,

"They divided my clothes among them
   and cast lots for my garment."

So this is what the soldiers did.

Near the cross of Jesus stood his mother, his mother's sister, Mary the wife of Clopas, and Mary Magdalene. When Jesus saw his mother there, and the disciple whom he loved standing near by, he said to her, "Woman, here is your son," and to the disciple, "Here is your mother." From that time on, this disciple took her into his home.

Later, knowing that everything had now been finished, and so that Scripture would be fulfilled, Jesus said, "I am thirsty." A jar of wine vinegar was there, so they soaked a sponge in it, put the sponge on a stalk of the hyssop plant, and lifted it to Jesus' lips. When he had received the drink, Jesus said, "It is finished." With that, he bowed his head and gave up his spirit.

Now it was the day of Preparation, and the next day was to be a special Sabbath. Because the Jewish leaders did not want the bodies left on the crosses during the Sabbath—Saturday, the Jewish weekly holy day—they asked Pilate to have the legs broken, because then the men would be unable to lift their bodies to breathe, and so would suffocate and die more quickly, and the bodies taken down. The soldiers therefore came and broke the legs of the first man who had been crucified with Jesus, and then those of the other. But when they came to Jesus and found that he was already dead, they did not break his legs. Instead, one of the soldiers pierced Jesus' side with a spear, bringing a sudden flow of what looked like blood and water. The man who saw it has given testimony, and his testimony is true. He knows that he tells the truth, and he testifies so that you also may believe. These things happened so that the scripture would be fulfilled: "Not one of his bones will be broken," and, as another scripture says, "They will look on the one they have pierced."

Later, Joseph of Arimathea asked Pilate for the body of Jesus. Now Joseph was a disciple of Jesus, but secretly because he feared the Jewish leaders. With Pilate's permission, he came and took the body away. He was accompanied by Nicodemus, a religious leader who earlier had visited Jesus at night, and as he asked about the kingdom of God, had been told: "God so loved the world that he gave his one and only Son, that whoever believes in him shall not perish but have eternal life". Nicodemus brought a mixture of myrrh and aloes, about thirty-five kilograms. Taking Jesus' body, the two of them wrapped it, with the spices, in strips of linen, to mask the smell of the corpse in the heat. This was in accordance with Jewish burial customs. At the place where Jesus was crucified, there was a garden, and in the garden a new tomb, in which no one had ever been laid. Because it was the Jewish day of Preparation for the Sabbath, and since the tomb was near by, they laid Jesus there.

READ THE FULL STORY John 19 v 16-42

▶ Why it really matters

There was nothing particularly abnormal about Jesus' crucifixion, in many ways. To our 21st-century Western ears, the details of crucifixion are shocking. The condemned man (women were executed in a relatively more humane way), who had already been tortured by flogging, would be stretched across the beam, probably having his shoulders dislocated in the process. Big nails would be driven through his wrists. The beam would be attached to a pole in the ground, and he would hang there, his feet either nailed to the wood or resting on a small ledge, and he would push himself up on the nails or ledge to breathe. Every breath was agony, but it often took days to die, usually of heart failure.

It was a cruel way to die—deliberately so. Crosses were mounted in the most public places, as a way of the Romans saying to their conquered subjects, *This is what happens if you oppose Rome. Do you really want to take us on?* The cross was meant to scare people; but it would not have shocked people. 2,000 years ago, crucifixions were a part of everyday life—not a pleasant one, but a normal one.

And so if you had been a first-century passer-by and had glanced at three men dying on crosses just outside Jerusalem, you wouldn't have given them much of a second glance, or very much thought. You'd have reacted as we do when a prison van drives past. We think, *I wonder who that is? I wonder what they've done?* and then we get on with our day.

You'd have seen a man carrying his cross-beam to his execution site; soldiers gambling to see who would keep the valuable items of clothing; a criminal touchingly ensuring his mother was cared for once he'd finally breathed his last, agonising breath; the man in the middle shouting something and then dying, surprisingly quickly; and then soldiers breaking the legs of the other two so that they died and could be taken down before the Sabbath day of rest.

This was an everyday event.

But if a passer-by had stopped and looked more closely at the man on the middle cross—at what happened around him, and what he said—they might have realised that this was, in fact, a death like no other.

Dead, according to plan

This death was according to a plan. It was a death that was chosen. And that is remarkable, because this was the most barbaric, most painful, most brutal form of death ever invented by mankind. Who plans to get nailed to a cross? Who chooses to die like this?

The answer lies in "the scripture"—the Old Testament portion of our Bibles. As John watched all that went on, he realised that it "happened that the scripture would be fulfilled". Through his prophets, God had laid out not only that his King would come and ride a donkey, but that his King would come and hang on a cross. And he had explained why his King would die this way. He had given three sets of clues that explain what was going on as Jesus died. In the rest of this chapter, we'll look at each clue.

Clue #1: the clothes

So as we take a close look at what is going on, the first thing to notice is that it is *Jesus'* clothes that are being competed for by the soldiers, by casting lots. And a millennium before, in a song (that we call Psalm 22), a king—King David of Israel—had spoken of an experience of being abandoned by God; of being rejected, mocked and defeated, and yet eventually proving victorious. And David had told of how at the moment of abandonment, his clothes had been divided among his enemies, who cast lots to claim them.

Now, as Jesus hangs on a cross, and his clothes are divided among the soldiers, John realises that David's words are a clue that explain what is going on: here is God's *ultimate* King, the all-powerful ruler promised through Zechariah; and that he has been utterly abandoned by God, but will somehow emerge victorious. Jesus is the King, separated from God. He is God the Son, abandoned by God the Father. Why?

Clue #2: the plant, the bones and the calendar

Again, the answer lies in "scripture". When Jesus said he was thirsty, they soaked a sponge in wine vinegar, "put the sponge on a stalk of the hyssop plant, and lifted it to Jesus' lips". Then, once he was dead, the soldiers went to break his legs, but he was already dead—and so they left his bones unbroken. John says that this "happened so that the scripture would be fulfilled: 'Not one of his bones will be broken'". If you want to know why God's

King was abandoned by God, you need to look at the plant, and the bones—and the calendar.

The week of Jesus' death was the week of the Jewish Passover festival. This was an annual event that remembered a historical episode (like Bonfire Night in the UK, or Independence Day in the US)—in this case, the "Passover". Centuries before, on a particular night in a particular place, God had rescued his people from oppression and death under the Egyptian emperor, the Pharaoh. He had done this at the same time as he judged every family in Egypt who had rejected him as God; in other words, every family who had sinned—which was every family. The judgment was that their firstborn son would die (you can read about this whole episode in the Old Testament book of Exodus, chapter 11 verse 1 to chapter 14 verse 31).

But God had also offered Israel, and anyone who joined in with them—a way for those sons to get through his judgment alive. Any family, he said, could take a lamb and kill it without breaking any of its bones, and that would be enough. The lamb didn't deserve judgment—the family did—but the lamb would take the judgment for them. If a lamb had died, the son would not need to die.

And then, God said, the family needed to take the blood of the lamb, and wipe it round their doorframe, to show that the family inside that house took God's judgment seriously, and trusted God's way out completely. God told them to wipe the blood on the door using nature's version of a paintbrush—a hyssop plant.

If that all sounds a bit strange, it's because it is! How could a lamb's death take the place of a person's death? And why all the details about not breaking the bones, and using a hyssop plant? Because it was all a picture of a greater rescue from a greater judgment.

After Jesus died, unlike the men crucified with him, his bones were not broken. And before Jesus died, he was wiped with hyssop.

And as Jesus died, he was suffering God's judgment of separation from him and everything good.

So as John looked at the cross, he realised "the scripture" was being fulfilled. In other words, he worked out that those lambs at the first Passover were another clue that explained what Jesus was doing at this Passover. He was like those lambs, dying undeservedly to take the judgment that others should face. He was experiencing life outside God's kingdom and tasting death so that others wouldn't have to. In Egypt, the lambs had taken the punishment for the people's sins so that those people could avoid death. On the cross, Jesus, the ultimate "lamb", took the punishment for people's sins so they could avoid eternity in hell.

The King whom we have rejected has served our sentence for us. In our sin, we do the crime. On the cross as he experienced hell, he did our time.

Clue #3: The pierced fountain

So what does all this mean? Again, John reaches back to "another scripture" to help himself, and us, to understand: "As another scripture says, 'They will look on the one they have pierced'". That's another prediction made through Zechariah—and John and the other Jewish watchers would have known how Zechariah had continued:

"They will look on me, the one they have pierced, and they will mourn for him as one mourns for an only child ... On that day a fountain will be opened to the house of David and the inhabitants of Jerusalem, to cleanse them from sin and impurity."   (Zechariah 12 v 10; 13 v 1)

As John watched the soldier stab the pierced body of Jesus, he saw a fountain of what looked like blood and water pour out. And another fountain had been opened, too—a fountain of spiritually-cleansing water that cleans more than feet, and cleans deeper than feet. As Jesus went through the death and punishment that we deserve, he poured out a "fountain" that can "cleanse ... from sin". This is water that can clean up our hearts, that can wipe away those diary entries of "Jesus is not my King. Take him away", and that can enable us to enjoy eternity in his kingdom rather than enduring eternity outside it. Here, John saw, was a fountain that anyone could wash in.

Peter and John had not understood what Jesus was doing as he washed their feet the night before. But now, as he stood in front of the crucified corpse of his King, John grasped it. This was no ordinary death—it was a unique one.

Jesus, God's King, God's own Son, had been separated from his Father for the first and only time in eternity, shut out of his own kingdom.

He had died as a sacrifice, like those Passover lambs, bearing that separation so that his people will never have to face it.

He had died to open up a fountain of cleansing.

Look closer

That's what John saw as he looked at the cross. It's not what most people noticed. Pilate was still in his palace, getting on with governing. The chief priests were busy being annoyed about the exact wording of the notice above Jesus' head. The soldiers were busy working out who would get a dead man's clothes.

Today, most people don't look at the cross at all, or they only glance briefly at it. But in this chapter, as you think about John's account, you are looking at it. What do you see? A waste? A tragedy? A failure? Look closer. Could it be the place—the only place—where you can find new life, a fresh start, a deep cleansing, an eternity of peace and freedom?

Do you see that man hanging, bleeding, suffering, dying on that cross, and see that he did it for *you*—he went through all that for *you*?

That's what John saw. But perhaps John was mistaken. Perhaps Jesus was mistaken. Anyone can claim to be a king. But this king is dead, and dead kings don't rule—it's hard to establish peace when you're lying lifeless in a tomb. You need to be alive to do that.

6. Sunday. Running and eating.

> What really happened

Early on the Sunday, while it was still dark, Mary Magdalene, one of Jesus' closest friends, went to the tomb and saw that the stone had been removed from the entrance. This was astonishing, and troubling—tombs had disc-like stones that rolled down a groove to cover the entrance. While easy to close a tomb, it was a big job to open it up again.

So Mary came running to Simon Peter and the other disciple, the one Jesus loved (that is, John), and said, "They have taken the Lord out of the tomb, and we don't know where they have put him!"

So Peter and the other disciple started for the tomb. Both were running, but the other disciple outran Peter and reached the tomb first. He bent over and looked in at the strips of linen lying there but did not go in. Then Simon Peter came along behind him and went straight into the tomb. He saw the strips of linen that Jesus' corpse had been wrapped in lying there, as well as the cloth that had been wrapped round Jesus' head. The cloth was still lying in its place, separate from the linen. Finally the other disciple, who had reached the tomb first, also went inside. He saw and believed what his eyes were telling him—that Jesus had risen. (They still did not understand from God's predictions in Scripture that Jesus had to rise from the dead.) Then the disciples went back to where they were staying. Now Mary stood outside the tomb crying. As she wept, she bent over to look into the tomb and saw two angels in white, seated where Jesus' body had been, one at the head and the other at the foot.

They asked her, "Woman, why are you crying?"

"They have taken my Lord away," she said, "and I don't know where they have put him." At this, she turned round and saw Jesus standing there, but she did not realise that it was Jesus.

He asked her, "Woman, why are you crying? Who is it you are looking for?"

Thinking he was the gardener, she said, "Sir, if you have carried my friend's body away, tell me where you have put him, and I will get him."

But it wasn't the gardener.

Jesus said to her, "Mary."

She turned towards him... looked at him... and, in the moment of amazed recognition, cried out, "Teacher!"

Jesus said, "Do not hold on to me, for I have not yet ascended to the Father. Go instead to my friends and tell them, 'I am ascending to my Father and your Father, to my God and your God.'"

Mary went to the disciples with the news: "I have seen the Lord!" And she told them that he had said these things to her.

Later that day, in the evening, when the disciples were together, with the doors locked for fear of the Jewish leaders, Jesus came and stood among them and said, "Peace be with you!" After he said this, he showed them his hands and side. The disciples were overjoyed when they saw the Lord.

Again Jesus said, "Peace be with you! As the Father has sent me, I am sending you." And with that he breathed on them and said, "Receive the Holy Spirit. If you forgive anyone's sins, their sins are forgiven; if you do not forgive them, they are not forgiven."

`READ THE FULL STORY` John 20 v 1-23

❯ Why it really matters

I don't have high standards for a film. Probably because I am a history geek, I like it to include some swords, some battles, and some good, cheesy lines.

And so *Gladiator* ticks all my boxes. Lots of swords, lots of battles, and lines like these:

"What we do in life echoes in eternity."

"On my command, unleash hell."

And then at the end, when the hero, Maximus, has killed the evil emperor in mortal combat to restore Rome to freedom and justice (or, if you were a conquered part of their empire like Israel, oppression and exploitation), but has himself died in the fight, the line:

"He was a soldier of Rome. Honour him."

And that, as the Roman senators and gladiators bear his corpse out of the Colosseum, is the end of Maximus and the end of the film.

Except that it isn't. Instead, we see Maximus, alive beyond his own death, in a cornfield, with his wife and child (already brutally murdered by the emperor) running towards him. We hear the friend who has been by his side for most of the film whispering:

"I will see you again. But not yet… not yet."

Only then does the film end.

Why did they add those last bits? Because something inside us is dissatisfied with death being the end. A life well lived… a heroic final deed… it's not enough. Deep down, we want there to be more. We long for a happy ever after, even as life repeatedly reminds us that death is the end. Of course we long for this—because if death is the end, then all our achievements and accumulations are useless. Death mocks all our ambitions and efforts. The full stop of death removes much of the point of life.

And so, though we live in a society that has increasingly rejected the idea of God and the truth of the Christian faith, we still don't talk about death as being the end. Instead, we talk about passing on, moving upstairs, becoming an angel or a star… anything to suggest that death is not the final scene.

Of course, all that could be wishful thinking—just another idea that death mocks. Or it could be because we were made to live without the interruption of death, and were designed for happy ever after.

If the Diary of Disciple John were turned into a film, it should finish with the hero's death. Even Jesus himself acknowledged: "It is finished". He receives an honourable burial, and then the credits roll.

Except they don't. There's time for two huge twists.

Disappeared

Here's the first—the body disappears. A grieving woman goes to pay her respects at her friend's tomb, a sad scene repeated countless times every day in our world. You may well know how it feels to stand at a loved one's grave for the first time—to feel that numb, raw grief, mixed with memories and diluted by disbelief.

But what you probably don't know is what it feels like to see that the grave is empty. Yet that's what Mary saw—the body had gone. She did what I would—she ran away to fetch someone else, someone who might tell her that her eyes were playing tricks on her.

They weren't. Simon Peter and John reach the tomb, and take in the scene. The strips of linen and the cloth used to wrap Jesus' head are where they should be.

But the body isn't.

Reappeared

Here's the second twist—the body reappears. Alive. Can you imagine the terror? "When the disciples were together … Jesus came and stood among them and said…" Here is a walking, talking Jesus. The King on the donkey had become a corpse in the tomb, just as the religious leaders had planned… but then he had become a living man whose death lay behind him, instead of ahead of him.

The first twist was unexpected, but not unheard of. Bodies do go missing. Mary herself thought that perhaps the gardener had moved it. The second twist was unexpected—the disciples were meeting behind locked doors because they were defeated, scared of their enemies, terrified they would be next to get nailed to a cross. But this second twist is utterly stunning—a living person had reappeared.

The biggest twist

If this were a film, it would be far-fetched. Dead people do not rise. Yet now John's diary has recorded two dead people rising—Lazarus, and Jesus. It sounds as unlikely as Maximus walking through a cornfield on the way to embrace his family beyond his death.

Except that here's the biggest twist. The claim about Jesus is true.

John was an eyewitness. He stood at the foot of the cross and watched his friend die. He was the second person to see the empty tomb. He "saw and believed", even though he still didn't grasp that the resurrection of Jesus from the dead was all part of the plan laid out by God in Scripture. But was he right to believe? Surely as he and Peter "went back to where they were staying" he must have wondered. A missing body does not equal a resurrection truth.

But then Mary came back. "I have seen the Lord!", she said. But was she right? Perhaps grief had played tricks on her?

Then, that evening, John saw with his eyes. He saw Jesus breathe. He heard Jesus speak. He looked at Jesus' hands and side—at the places where the nails and then the spear had torn his flesh. This man was alive, and this man was the crucified Jesus. Now John knew: because a living body does equal a resurrection truth.

It still sounds unlikely, doesn't it? After all, John had a great interest in writing this final scene. A few scribbles of his pen and his friend Jesus, who he'd thought was God's chosen King, would no longer be a criminal, crushed by Rome, but a hero, raised by God. And John would no longer have made a terrible error of judgement in following him, but would be a man of power and influence, the friend of the Christ.

Except... that didn't happen. By the time John wrote up his account, decades had passed; and in those decades most of the men who were in that locked room on that Sunday evening had been killed—beheaded, crucified, stoned—for saying that Jesus had risen from the dead. By the time John published his account and insisted that it should be placed on the biography shelves, not in the fiction section, he had nothing to gain and everything to lose from writing what he did. He faced not power and influence, but prison and infamy.

Yet still he wrote. Still he listed the proofs. Still he said, *I saw him. He's alive.* Still he speaks to us over the centuries and says, *This is not a fairy story to make you feel better. This is not an extra scene to round the film off. This is a fact of history—and it changes your life, your future, your world.*

The difference it makes

What difference does the resurrection make? First, it means peace is available. Jesus' first word to his subjects after he's risen is, "Peace". He's so keen for them to grasp what he's offering that he repeats himself, "Peace be with you!" Remember who he's speaking to. He's speaking to those who had misunderstood him, who had committed violence in his name, and most of whom had run away instead of being there for him at his bitter end. But he doesn't come to them to say, "Why did you let me down?" or "I hope you're sorry". No—he comes to them and says, "Peace".

That's who Jesus is. He's the all-powerful, all-encompassing King who offers peace terms to a world that has said: *Take him away!* He is so powerful that death couldn't defeat him. He rules eternity. Peace with him is advisable. Wonderfully, peace with him is available.

Second, Jesus' resurrection means he is present with his subjects. As he breathed on his friends, he said, "Receive the Holy Spirit". One of the deepest truths Jesus revealed was that there is one God, in three persons—a united, unique royal family of the universe. The Father, Son and Spirit are all fully God, but each different from one another. The Father had sent the Son to the world to announce his rule and to die for his people. Now the Father had raised the Son to offer peace terms and to give the Spirit to those who accepted those terms.

Jesus was giving God himself to his disciples. Soon, he would return to heaven, so his subjects would not have God's Son on earth, living among them. Instead, they would have something even better—God's Spirit living in them. They would never be alone, powerless, helpless or hopeless. Their King would be present within them each day of their life until they moved into his presence on the last day of their life.

Third, Jesus' resurrection means it is possible to live with purpose. When Jesus told his friends, "If you forgive anyone's sins, their sins are forgiven; if you do not forgive them, they are not forgiven", he wasn't giving them the power that only he has—the power to give a royal pardon. He was telling them to tell people that a royal pardon is possible. It was their task to tell others that if they trusted Jesus' death, then they were forgiven, at peace with God, and part of his eternal kingdom; and that if they did not, then there was no forgiveness, no peace, and they were not part of the kingdom.

Everyone needs a purpose. When we get up in the morning, we all want to build something—a relationship, a career, a reputation, a list of experiences. The problem is that, whatever we build, death takes it away. In 200 years, very little of what we built will be remembered by others and none of it will matter to us... unless our purpose is to proclaim Jesus' offer of peace and presence. That is something that death does not take away, because the King has defeated death already. You can do something that will still matter, and will still be celebrated, in 200, 2,000 and 2,000,000 years, and that matters to you more than anything else.

There is a point to life: and it is to accept the offer of life in the next one, and to tell others about it. You're probably reading this book because someone knows that that's the point, and they told you about King Jesus, and encouraged you to read this book. That's the point.

Another scene

A few years ago, I spoke at my grandad's funeral. We'd been very close when I was a child, and I miss him terribly. I'd love for my children to have met him.

As I stood before his coffin, everything in me wanted there to be another scene to his life, for this not to be the end, for death not to have the final word and blot out all that this man was and did.

So everything in me wanted to believe that there would be a happy ever after for Grandad.

But wonderfully, I didn't have to resort to wishful thinking, to clichés about him now being a star in the sky, looking down on us as he played heavenly golf, and so on.

I could rest on historical fact. As I looked at Grandad's coffin, heading for his grave, I could know that his death had already been taken, and defeated, in another grave. Because he had known and trusted that Jesus had died to open the way into his kingdom, and had risen to invite him in, I could know Grandad was alive beyond his own death.

I could look at the coffin and finish my talk by saying, "See you soon, Grandad". I said that not only because I so desperately want it to be true, but because it is true. The resurrection of Jesus is a place where what we long for and what is real wonderfully collide. Jesus has risen. And so there can be an extra scene, even beyond death.

7. A few days later. Gone fishing...

▶ What really happened

Jesus appeared again to his disciples, by the Sea of Galilee, the place which many of them had called home before they met him. It happened this way: Simon Peter, Thomas (also known as Didymus), Nathanael from Cana in Galilee, the sons of Zebedee (James and John), and two other disciples were together.

"I'm going out to fish," Simon Peter told them, and they said, "We'll go with you." So they went out and got into the boat, but that night they caught nothing.

Early in the morning, Jesus stood on the shore, but the disciples did not realise that it was Jesus.

He called out to them, "Friends, haven't you any fish?"

"No," they answered.

He said, "Throw your net on the right side of the boat and you will find some." When they did, they were unable to haul the net in because of the large number of fish.

Then the disciple whom Jesus loved said to Peter, "It is the Lord!" When they landed, they saw a fire of burning coals there with fish on it, and some bread.

Jesus said to them, "Bring some of the fish you have just caught." So Simon Peter climbed back into the boat and dragged the net ashore. It was full of large fish, 153, but even with so many the net was not torn. Jesus said to them, "Come and have breakfast."

When they had finished eating, Jesus said to Simon Peter, "Simon son of John, do you love me more than these?"

The last time Simon Peter had been asked a question about Jesus had been as he stood by another fire. That time, the questioner had been a servant-girl, not the King of the world. It had been on the night of Jesus' arrest, while he was on trial for his life...

"You aren't one of this man's disciples too, are you?" she asked Peter.

He replied, "I am not."

It was cold, and the servants and officials stood round a fire they had made to keep warm. Peter also was standing with them, warming himself.

So they asked him, "You aren't one of Jesus' disciples too, are you?"

He denied it, saying, "I am not."

One of the high priest's servants challenged him, "Didn't I see you with him in the garden?"

Again Peter denied it...

Now, on the beach, the friend he had been so quick to deny wanted an answer. "Do you love me?"

"Yes, Lord," Peter said, "you know that I love you."

Jesus said, "Feed my lambs."

Again Jesus said, "Simon son of John, do you love me?"

He answered, "Yes, Lord, you know that I love you."

Jesus said, "Take care of my sheep."

The third time he said to him, "Simon son of John, do you love me?"

Peter was hurt because Jesus asked him the third time, "Do you love me?" He said, "Lord, you know all things; you know that I love you."

Jesus said, "Feed my sheep. Very truly I tell you, when you were younger you dressed yourself and went where you wanted; but when you are old you will stretch out your hands, and someone else will dress you and lead you where you do not want to go." Jesus said this to indicate the kind of death by which Peter would glorify God—a death that would involve stretching out his hands, and that he would not welcome; a death on a cross, like his King's.

Then Jesus said to him, "Follow me!"

Peter turned and saw that the disciple whom Jesus loved was following them. This is the disciple who testifies to these things and who wrote them down.

READ THE FULL STORY John 21 v 1-24; 18 v 15-18, 25-27

❯ Why it really matters

Elton John once sang, "What do I say when it's all over? Sorry seems to be the hardest word."

In fact, sorry is a really easy word to say. It's only two syllables. But sorry is a very hard word to mean.

And it's the same with the words "I love you". They're so very easy to say. Millions of people will utter them round the world today. Some will do it thoughtfully: some not. Some will mean it: some won't. Some will really be saying, "I love me" or "I love you for now" or "I love you as long as you..."

To truly love someone is to put your heart in their hands, and to allow them to break it if they choose. It is to invest your future in theirs, so that your happiness is staked on what they do. It is to commit to putting them first, even when that's hard. It is to take a huge risk.

"I love you" is very easy to say. It is far harder to mean, and to live out.

Days before Jesus' death, John had seen love, as Mary gave the best thing she had to Jesus, because she was convinced that he was worth it. And now, days after Jesus' resurrection, John listens in on a conversation about love.

Three times, Jesus asks Peter, "Do you love me?" It's astonishing that Jesus even asks or cares—that he'll speak to Peter at all. The last time Jesus heard Peter speak, it was to hear him say, *I don't know him.* But Jesus is the King who serves, and he had promised to wash Peter clean of his dirt, even the filth of his denial. And, on the cross, Jesus had done it. So now he wants to know: does Peter love him?

And three times, Peter replies, "I love you".

What else could he say? He'd seen Jesus ride into Jerusalem on a donkey, declaring that he is the King who will rule everywhere, for ever. He'd seen Jesus wash his feet, declaring that he is the King who slaves for his people. He'd seen Jesus hang on a cross to bear his death, to take the punishment for his own moments where he had said, *I don't know him... Take him away!* He'd seen Jesus defeat death and offer him, even him, his peace and his presence.

He'd seen it all. He'd seen what kind of King his friend was. What else could he say? What else can anyone say?

I love you.

Love *does*

But Jesus isn't finished with his conversation, because "I love you" is easy to say, but the truth of the claim is only seen by how we live. Love says, and then love does. When people get married, at their wedding they speak their love, but they also promise their love. And it is married life rather than the wedding day where the reality of their love is seen, or not seen.

So Jesus wants to tell Peter, and anyone else who is thinking of knowing, loving and following Jesus, what love does.

First, love sticks. Why does Jesus ask Peter the same question three times? Because Peter had denied knowing him three times. Jesus is deliberately pointing Peter back to his moments of denial and saying, *Love doesn't do that. Love sticks.* Love is not a one-off, it's not even a three-off—it's a lifetime. We don't love Jesus if we do it part-time, when it's easy or popular but not when it's hard or costly. *You say I love you*, Jesus says to Peter. *Well, love sticks.*

Second, love recognises. Peter does not call Jesus his friend, his teacher, or even his master. He calls him "Lord". Peter has seen this man claim to be a King, he has watched him raise people from the dead, he has witnessed his own triumph over death and he has heard him give God's Spirit. He knows who Jesus is: God the Son, God the King.

To recognise Jesus as being anything less than the Lord, our King, is to reject him. Calling Jesus a teacher, a prophet or a guru is like a husband saying to his wife, *From now on, you're not my wife. You're my cleaner. Here's your money—now please do the dusting. Thank you.* That is not love—it's rejection. Love recognises who someone is. And so to love Jesus is to recognise him as "Lord".

Third, love cares. Jesus has shown his own care in how he died for his subjects. Now he gives Peter the job of "feeding" his "lambs"—of looking after his people. Peter will show his love for Jesus by caring about his people. If we truly love, we are not in it for ourselves. We give, not to get back, but because we love. Love cares.

Fourth, love costs. One day, Peter will face his own cross. And at that moment, his love will be proved because his love will cost him. Maybe you don't tend to talk about love because it's mushy, sentimental, about flowers and pet-names and debating who will hang up the phone first, and you've had enough of that. But that's not the love that Jesus is talking about. This is a love that is brave, courageous, uncompromising—the kind of love that sees soldiers dive on a grenade to save their comrades and that sees a mother take a bullet for her child. Peter needs to know that to love Jesus, to follow him as King, will cost him not just his wealth, as it cost Mary hers; it will cost him his life.

Round the world as you read these words, many men and women who love Jesus are following Peter, going to death because they love Jesus. Countless more are putting their bank balances, their calendars, their relationship dreams, their time and energy and emotions, at his disposal. Why? Because he's worth it. Because they love him—and love costs.

Do you…?

So when Peter says, *I love you*, he is saying a lot more than three simple words. He is saying to Jesus, *I am going to stick with you. I am going to recognise who you are. I am going to care for your people. I am going to accept the costs of following you. I love you.*

Why would he say that? Why does anyone say, and mean, I love you? It's because we know who we're saying it to. And Peter knew who he was walking along the seashore with—someone who loved him more than Peter would ever love him back. Jesus had stuck with Peter, recognised him, cared for him, and paid the ultimate, unimaginable cost for him. Jesus loved him.

In a sense, the same question is asked of all of us. How do you feel about Jesus? Do you love him?

It's the great challenge of the resurrection. Jesus doesn't want your mere acceptance that these things are true. He isn't satisfied if you simply understand why these things matter.

He wants your heart. He says to you, *I am ready to love you.*

Do you love me?

Another diary

In many ways, my diary from when I was 19 records a month of dull, repetitive life. It's quite boring to read, even for me.

But in one crucial way, it is not boring at all, because it records the month my life changed utterly, for ever.

Growing up, I'd always felt that Jesus probably existed, and that he probably died and rose. If I was asked, I'd have said he was God's Son. If pushed, I'd have called myself a Christian.

But I didn't understand that I needed Jesus. I didn't accept that my sin meant I should be shut out of his amazing kingdom, or that his death and resurrection meant I could be invited in. I didn't love him.

But in that month that I happened to keep a diary, it keeps telling of how a friend regularly came round to my room. He was called Martyn, and he was into climbing, comedy gags... and Christianity.

Martyn loved Jesus. He wasn't perfect, and he knew it, but he knew he'd been cleaned by Jesus and that he had peace, freedom and life with Jesus. So he didn't live like the rest of us. He didn't do the student lifestyle. And he was much happier than I was. He seemed (and I wouldn't have used this word at the time) blessed.

My diary records how we kept talking about Jesus. I write about how he gently but firmly told me how my life was being lived in rejection of Jesus as King. I write about how he invited me along to his church, but I didn't think I'd go. I write about how Martyn mentioned that Jesus tells us not to get drunk, and how I was going to ignore Martyn.

I write about how, for some reason, getting drunk has started to seem a silly way to find happiness when it just causes headaches. I write about how I have gone along to Martyn's church, and I have realised that Jesus is the King, and I am outside his kingdom, and he died to let me in, and how I think I need to come in.

I write about how I came to love Jesus—a love that, with Jesus' help, would stick, would recognise, would care and would cost.

So among the dull daily details of a normal student life—late nights, late mornings, work crises, relationship issues, money shortages—I was writing (though I didn't know it at the time) about the days when my life was transformed and my eternity changed. I was writing about the moments when I first said to King Jesus, *Thank you for bringing me into your eternal kingdom. I love you.*

Maybe reading this book has done something similar for you to what Martyn did for me. As you've read John's diary of that week of his life, you've come face to face with the real Jesus. You've seen that he's more powerful, more wonderful, more challenging and more compelling than you'd ever realised.

Maybe you need to do some more thinking about his claims and his offer. If that's you, there are some suggestions for how you could do that on page 67.

But maybe you know who Jesus was, and is. You know that the invisible line on every day of your diary has read: *Jesus is not my King. Take him away.* But you also know he died and rose for you. You know that following him as King will cost you everything you have, but also give you everything you need.

What's the date today? Maybe it's the date when you need to hear King Jesus asking you,

Do you love me?

And you need to answer:

Lord, I love you.

As he wrote his account of the last week of Jesus' life, John was hoping you would say that. He tells us that he wrote his Gospel, though it cost him his freedom and endangered his life, so "that you may believe that Jesus is the Messiah"—the Jewish word for King—"the Son of God, and that by believing you may have life in his name" (John 20 v 31).

Do you need to speak to Jesus the Messiah, the Son of God, right now?

What next?

Thanks for reading this book. I hope you've enjoyed it, and that it's informed and even excited you about Jesus.

I'm guessing you fall into one of two categories:

Maybe you're **someone who would like to keep looking into Christianity** before making your mind up about what you believe. Here are a few ways you can keep thinking things through...

Read a Gospel. There are four historical biographies of Jesus' life found in the Bible—John (the one this book is based on), Matthew, Mark and Luke. Why not grab one and read through it? The shortest one is Mark, which takes around two hours to read.

Pray. That may seem strange! But why not speak to God, and ask him, if he is there, to help you to see the truth about who he is, who Jesus is, and what life is all about?

Go to a website. *www.christianityexplored.org* allows you to keep thinking about Jesus in your own way, at your own pace, in your own time. It features an animation which explains who Jesus is, why he came, and what it means for us; some video answers to questions lots of people ask; and some real-life stories of people who thought things through themselves. And on the site, you can also find out about how you can...

Join a *Christianity Explored* course. This is an informal, relaxed, seven-week walk through Mark's Gospel, where you can ask questions, discuss or simply listen. You can find a course near you on the website.

Look at the historical evidence. If you'd like to look in more detail at how we know that the Gospels are real history, a great book to read is *The Case for Christ*, by Lee Strobel. You can get a copy at www.thegoodbook.co.uk/case-for-christ or at other online book-sellers.

Maybe, though, you're reading this page as *someone who has accepted Jesus as your King and asked him for a place in his kingdom*—you've become a Christian. That's fantastic! It can all seem a bit strange at first (or at least, it did for me). The best advice I can give you is to **find a church** near you that bases all it says and does on the Bible (in the same way this book does). The people there will help you get on with enjoying knowing Jesus, your Ruler and Rescuer, and encourage you to see how you can worship him. If you'd like a hand with finding a church like this, just email info@ thegoodbook.co.uk.

Yes, but...
isn't this all made up?

When you read something, it helps to know what you're reading. I wouldn't use a car manual to tell me how to cook a roast dinner; I wouldn't use a recipe book to help me change my car's oil!

Throughout this book, you'll have seen me talking about what the John's "Gospel" in the Bible tells us about Jesus. And I talk about what he says as though these things really happened; as though they were history. Why?

Because that's the type of books the Gospels are. They are eye-witness accounts. Matthew and John were some of Jesus' closest friends; Mark was written by a man who became a Christian within years of Jesus' death, and knew the eyewitnesses. Luke acted like a modern-day historian, interviewing eye-witnesses and putting together a biography (you can read how he put together his Gospel in the first few sentences of that Gospel).

Here's how John put it, in a letter he wrote towards the end of his life: **"That which ... we have heard, which we have seen with our eyes, which we have looked at and our hands have touched—this we proclaim"** (1 John 1 v 1). In other words: *I'm writing about what I've seen and heard. I was there.*

He, and Luke and Matthew and Mark, were writing historical biographies of Jesus' life. That's their claim.

Now of course, John and the others could have just made it all up, just as I could rewrite history to make my dad a Premier League star instead of a retired computing teacher. But it's completely unlikely that John would have done that, for two reasons.

First, at the time John and the other Gospel authors were writing their historical biographies of Jesus, you could very easily get killed for being a Christian. Why make up something that could land you in prison, facing torture and death?! It would be like me making up a back-story for my dad which claimed that he was a high-level ISIL terrorist, and that I was working for him.

Second, John was a Christian. It's easy to think that'd make it more likely that he'd make his Gospel up. Actually, it makes it less likely. If John thought this guy Jesus was God, he'd really, really care about getting the facts about him correct. He wouldn't want to make mistakes about someone so important. He'd be more careful to tell historical fact, not less.

One final thing that can make us even more confident that John and the others are telling us historical facts is that their stories fit with other historical accounts of the time. The events they talk about fit with other histories. The people they talk about, like Roman emperors and Jewish priests, are real people. Jesus himself is mentioned by both Roman and Jewish historians who would probably rather he hadn't lived; so he himself definitely existed. And the details of the places they wrote about, like how there were two towns next to each other with the same name, check out with archaeological research.

Which means that the Gospels claim to be historical fact; they sound like historical fact; and they check out with other histories as historical fact. Which is why, in this book, I treat what they say about Jesus as historical fact. Strange facts, amazing facts, challenging facts, but still facts!

If you'd like to think in more detail about why we can be confident that the Gospels are history, a couple of great books to read are: *Can we trust what the Gospels say about Jesus?* (you can get a copy at www.thegoodbook.co.uk/trust-jesus-gospels)
The Case for Christ (www.thegoodbook.co.uk/case-for-christ)

Yes, but...
surely Jesus didn't really rise?

One of Jesus' earliest followers, Paul, wrote that, **"If Christ has not been raised ... faith is useless"** *.

The resurrection of Jesus back to life is the place where the whole of Christianity stands or falls. And the resurrection of Jesus is the place where lots of people say, "That's just ridiculous. The rest of the story, OK—but not a dead man coming back to life!"

Let's be clear. No one can prove beyond any doubt that Jesus rose from the dead. But that's because no one can prove anything beyond any doubt. I can't prove my wife loves me—but, based on the evidence, I believe that she does. You can't prove that you're not a butterfly who's dreaming it's a human—but, based on the evidence, you believe that you're not (hopefully!).

So in thinking about whether Jesus rose or not, it's about what you think is the *most likely* explanation for what happened that day in history.

And people have come up with some pretty good explanations. Over the page are the best I've found. For each, I've laid out the explanation as well as I can, and then mentioned the questions that they don't really answer.

* 1 Corinthians 15 v 17 *(New English Translation Bible version)*

1. There was no empty tomb: the women went to the wrong one

The women were tired and upset when they saw where Jesus was laid. When they visited the body a couple of days later, they went to the wrong tomb. The body wasn't there, they put two and two together and made 648, and told everyone he'd been raised.

Unanswered questions:

- They weren't expecting him to rise. If you went to the wrong tomb, wouldn't you just find the right one, not announce a resurrection?!

- When Jesus' followers announced a month or so later that Jesus had risen, why didn't the authorities simply go to the tomb they'd put soldiers outside, get the body, and disprove the resurrection?

2. The tomb was empty because Jesus wasn't really dead

Jesus didn't die on the cross—he just fainted, and then came round in the cool tomb. He then spent time with his friends and ate and walked with them, and then went away and lived somewhere else. His friends assumed he'd gone to heaven, and started talking about the resurrection.

Unanswered questions:

- The Romans were good at crucifying people. Did they really think Jesus was dead when he wasn't?

- One of the soldiers near the cross stuck a spear into his side. Could a man who'd been stabbed in the heart survive without medical help for three days and then walk out?

- Could a man who'd been nailed to a cross go for a long walk with friends two days later?

- Why didn't the guards at the tomb notice Jesus limping out?

3. The tomb was empty because the body was taken by the authorities

The leaders knew Jesus had predicted his resurrection. So they moved the body to make sure there could be no scam. That left an empty tomb; and the disciples took advantage of this, or misunderstood this, and went round saying Jesus had risen.

Unanswered questions:

• If the authorities had the body, why didn't they produce it when people started believing Jesus had risen? That would have stopped the rumours of resurrection!

4. The tomb was empty because the body was taken by grave-robbers

Bodies weren't valuable, but grave-clothes were. So some grave-robbers stole the body. The tomb was left empty for the women to find, and a legend was born.

Unanswered questions:

• Why, when the empty tomb was discovered, were the valuable grave-clothes still there? Why hadn't the grave-robbers taken the only thing in the tomb of value?

5. The tomb was empty because the body was taken by the disciples

Jesus' followers had much to gain from a "resurrection". So they stole the body, announced the resurrection and said Jesus had appeared to them several times, and that he'd now gone away again, back to heaven. And the resurrection lie enabled them to set up a new religion—Christianity.

Unanswered questions:

• Could the disciples, who were terrified and had run away, really have managed to pull off stealing a body from under the noses of some Roman guards?

- If the disciples had made up the Gospels of Jesus in the Bible, why do they come across in them as scared, disloyal and weak? Wouldn't you write more impressive lies about yourself?

- If the disciples made this up, they knew for a fact Jesus hadn't risen. Yet almost all of them ended up being killed for saying he'd come back to life and was God. Wouldn't at least one of them have admitted it was all made up to avoid being crucified, stoned or beheaded?

6. The disciples didn't really see Jesus: it was a hallucination

The "appearances" of Jesus were simple hallucinations. After all, the disciples were emotional, tired and grieving—and they saw what they wanted to see.

Unanswered questions:

- Medically, people simply don't hallucinate the same thing at the same time. Did dozens (and on one occasion hundreds) of adults really have an identical hallucination at the same time?

- Why was the tomb empty? If this was a hallucination, the body would still have been in the tomb.

7. The tomb was empty because Jesus had risen back to life

This is what Jesus' friends claimed had happened, even when they faced gruesome deaths for saying it. It explains the empty tomb; and it explains the appearances of Jesus after his death.

Unanswered questions:

- Do people really rise from the dead? It's not exactly a normal event! (To which my answer, for what it's worth, is that if you were God, you could raise someone from the dead without difficulty. And if you wanted to prove you were God, you'd need to do something amazing and abnormal—like promising to die and rise again, and then actually doing that.)

EVERYONE HAS A PICTURE OF JESUS.
Why not meet the real one?

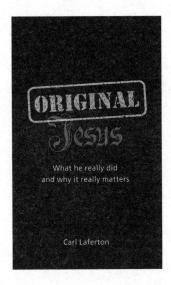

ORIGINAL JESUS

Carl Laferton

"Lively and engaging, this book makes clear who Jesus is—and why we need him. A great introduction to the true Jesus."

Gavin Peacock, ex-English Premier League midfielder with Chelsea and Newcastle

thegoodbook.com/oj

the**good**book

COMPANY

Opening up the Bible

Thanks for reading this book. We hope you enjoyed it, and found it helpful.

Most people want to find answers to the big questions of life: Who are we? Why are we here? How should we live? But for many valid reasons we are often unable to find the time or the right space to think positively and carefully about them.

Perhaps you have questions that you need an answer for. Perhaps you have met Christians who have seemed unsympathetic or incomprehensible. Or maybe you are someone who has grown up believing, but need help to make things a little clearer.

At The Good Book Company, we're passionate about producing materials that help people of all ages and stages understand the heart of the Christian message, which is found in the pages of the Bible.

Whoever you are, and wherever you are at when it comes to these big questions, we hope we can help. As a publisher we want to help you look at the good book that is the Bible because we're convinced that as we meet the person who stands at its centre—Jesus Christ—we find the clearest answers to our biggest questions.

Visit our website to discover the range of books, videos and other resources we produce, or visit our partner site www.christianityexplored. org for a clear explanation of who Jesus is and why he came.

Thanks again for reading,

Your friends at The Good Book Company

UK & EUROPE   thegoodbook.co.uk   0333 123 0880
NORTH AMERICA   thegoodbook.com   866 244 2165
AUSTRALIA   thegoodbook.com.au   (02) 6100 4211
NEW ZEALAND   thegoodbook.co.nz   (+64) 3 343 2463

WWW.CHRISTIANITYEXPLORED.ORG
Our partner site is a great place for those exploring the Christian faith, with a clear explanation of the good news, powerful testimonies and answers to difficult questions.